DR. MARCEL'S

LITTLE BOOK OF

BIG LOVE

DR. MARCEL'S

LITTLE BOOK OF

BIG LOVE

YOUR GUIDE TO FINDING LOVE, THE ISLAND WAY

BLINK

bringing you closer

Published by Blink Publishing
3.08, The Plaza,
535 Kings Road,
Chelsea Harbour,
London, SW10 0SZ

www.blinkpublishing.co.uk

facebook.com/blinkpublishing
twitter.com/blinkpublishing

Hardback – 978-1-78870-01-46
Ebook – 978-1-788700-09-2

A CIP catalogue of this book is available from the British Library.

Designed by seagulls.net
Printed and bound by Clays Ltd, St Ives Plc

1 3 5 7 9 10 8 6 4 2

Blink Publishing is an imprint of the Bonnier Publishing Group
www.bonnierpublishing.co.uk

This book is dedicated to my family and friends who have always shown me so much love. And for Gabs, who made my time in Love Island so special. I love you all.

INTRODUCTION

I've written a book. About, like, love and stuff. I'm not saying I'm some kind of love guru or anything. Nah, scrap that, I am. Because let's face it, who knows more about romance than Dr. Marcel?

I had such a wicked time on *Love Island* and somehow along the way I became the villa's official love doctor. I didn't set out to dispense relationship advice but with so many people having issues in there I didn't have much choice. And having dated a lot of girls in my time I know what I'm talking about.

So this is my way of passing all my years of dating knowledge on to you and I really hope you enjoy it.

BIG love,

Marcel X

LET'S TALK ABOUT SEX (AND ME!)

*L*et's get the basics out of the way first. Why did I decide to do *Love Island*? What fit geezer wouldn't want to do it? Basically, I watched it last year and thought, 'I want a bit of that.'

I knew I'd be good in the show because I'm positive and upbeat and I like a laugh, and I knew whatever happened it would be fun. But for me it was mainly about trying to meet the right girl. I'd been looking around thinking, 'Where is she?' Then I decided she might just be on the island, lying on a sun lounger in a bikini.

I was looking for a girl that was confident, funny and up for banter. And she had to have curves. I love curves on a girl. What I didn't want was someone arrogant, argumentative or pleased with themselves. All those traits are a massive turn-off for me.

I haven't got a type but I'm basically making it my life's mission to find someone who is a cross between Shakira, Gemma Arterton and my all-time favourite woman, Julia Roberts. Is that too specific? Okay then, I'll settle for a big smile. I've got a pretty big smile and I like a girl who mirrors that. You can't beat someone whose face lights up when they're happy.

None of my ex-girlfriends have looked the same. My first girlfriend was petite and curvy with blonde hair and green eyes, and the girlfriend I was with for seven years was mixed race with brown eyes, so I guess I like to mix things up a bit.

It wasn't like I had been single for ages and I was desperate when I went into *Love Island*. I'd only been single for a year, tops.

I've had girlfriends since I was three years old at nursery school. Even then I was irresistible. I got together with my first proper girlfriend when I was 14. It was all pretty innocent and we just went to the cinema and stuff. Then when I was 15 or 16 I went out with my first serious girlfriend and lost my virginity.

I saw a few other girls here and there after we split up and then I went out with a girl on and off for seven years, which is a pretty heavy commitment at that age.

We were together while I was in the band (I don't like to talk about it but I used to be in Blazin' Squad) so it was quite hard because we did have girls throwing themselves at us all the time. I remember going on the *Smash Hits* tour and there were crowds of girls outside our hotel 24/7. Some of them even used to book themselves into rooms so they could try and get close to us. It was mad.

Although I definitely had the opportunity to pull other girls I was always really loyal to my girlfriend. We'd have times where we split up for a month or two and during that time I would meet new girls and have a bit of fun.

My girlfriend and I split up for a year once and I ended up seeing someone else for a lot of that time and we definitely had something, but we broke up because I was so busy with the band and travelling all over the country, so it was hard to lock down anything solid. I never knew where I'd be from one week to the next so it wasn't the best time to be starting something new.

Looking back, I think that's the reason the seven-year relationship lasted for so long. We kept breaking up and getting back together because we had an understanding and we both knew that things would be up and down sometimes. She got that I was on the road a lot and I couldn't be like a 'normal' boyfriend and take her out every weekend. She knew things were never going to be straightforward, and because we got on well and we liked each other we kept drifting back together.

We split for good when I was 23 and it was really hard. Young love is never easy, and we'd been in each other's lives for such a long time. I guess you think you'll never get over your first ex because it's all new to you.

Having said that, it was after we split up that I went through my hot patch and I was never without female company. I was living life and going out partying every night while still doing shows with the band, so it was a pretty non-stop situation, if you get my drift. But not as non-stop as it's been made out to be.

I'll hold my hands up; I did put it out there that I've had sex with between 200 and 300 women. But everyone's taken the 300 and run with it. Now people are like, 'Did you know that Marcel bloke from *Love Island* has slept with 300 women?' and it sounds a bit bad. So I'll clear that up now: it was somewhere between 200 and 300, not over 300. You've got to leave time for other things in your life.

To be fair, back in the day it wasn't the life I chose, it was the life that chose me. Anyone would have done the same if they were in the same position as me. I have slowed down now. Not because I'm getting old. I'm just wiser, innit.

ISLAND
LIFE

*T*he first day of *Love Island* was not what I was expecting at all. When you walk in it is pretty daunting. You're being judged and you want to be liked. That's human nature.

I was the first to go in which was scary, man. And all the girls were gorgeous, and for the first time in my life I felt a bit overwhelmed. Then when no one stepped forward for me I was thinking, 'Oh my god, I've ruined my life. All my friends are watching this. And my mum's watching and she's probably panicking for me.'

I actually couldn't believe it when no one stepped forward. What's up with that? Looks-wise I'm a 9.9, and personality-wise I'm a 10. How can they not love this face? It's a good face. And I'm an ex-pop star too. Have I mentioned that?

Amber said she thought I was too confident, but when did that become a thing? If she'd said she was intimidated by my handsomeness, I would have understood. But the path of true love never runs smooth (Shakespeare said that and he was nearly as clued up about love as I am).

After that dodgy beginning, I managed to totally turn things around. Eventually everyone realised how much of a nice person I actually am. Everyone warmed to me and it was really good because it was like, 'Yeah, now everyone realises I'm a proper gent and I'm a lovely dude.'

I always try to be a good guy. Like when I had to tell some of the girls that their nipples had popped out during the twerking challenge. I couldn't just stand by and watch it happening. I'm not sure all the male viewers at home thanked me for it, but it was the right thing to do.

As I mentioned before, I didn't set out to become everyone's shoulder to cry on, but it naturally happened. It all started just before Harley left. He took someone else's advice about going to speak to Chloe and then she ended up ditching him. Afterwards I told him it was the worst advice ever and I gave him some better advice, and that was that. After that evening, everyone started coming to me and asking for help when they were upset or confused. People also came to me if they were feeling sad, and I became the in-house doctor/dad. It was mad.

Every single person in the villa got a hug from me at some point. Even when Liv and I had a massive argument I was still giving her hugs because I wanted there to be a nice atmosphere. I tried to treat people how I like to be treated.

I was happy to sit and listen to anyone and I
enjoyed it. I was always open for business. You
do need a shoulder to lean on in the villa, and I
became everyone's shoulder. That helped me get
through it too. Making other people happy makes
me feel happy.

Seeing people go from crying to smiling made me
feel so good.

Cam used to cry all the time because she's very
sweet and sensitive, but she knew I always had her
back. She knew she could come to me any time and
she always got the biggest hugs.

People came to me because I was pretty much
always positive and I had a positive outlook no
matter how bad the situation was. Dishing out
advice came pretty naturally to me because I already
do it with my friends on the outside. My mates
know that if they ever need to talk about anything,
I'll give them good, solid advice.

I did think the same thing might happen in the
villa, but at the same time I didn't want to be all
like, 'Yeah, I'm great, come and talk to me any
time you've got a problem.' I didn't build myself a
little surgery in the garden and sit there with a pen

and paper waiting to take notes. It just happened naturally. I'm good at explaining what I'm thinking and why I'm thinking it and I'm straightforward with things. I think people appreciated that.

There were so many ups and downs in the villa and it could be intense at times. I think I probably helped a few relationships in there; even some of the couples that were in the final. I gave them the guidance they needed in order for them to move things forward.

My *Love Island* experience definitely wasn't all plain sailing for me. There was a moment in week five or six where I felt like I'd been drained of all my positivity. I said to Gabs, 'You know what, for this week I'm just going to spend all my time with you. I'm not going to give anyone advice. I need to focus on myself and get my energy back up.'

It was hard because I wanted to be there for everyone else, and when I hit a wall I didn't know who to talk to about it. There were times when I needed advice and I was like, 'Paging Dr. Marceeeeeel.' But it didn't work because I can't page myself, innit?

I can chat to myself in my head but it's not the same.

Thankfully feeling rubbish didn't last long. I soon pulled myself out of it and started going back to helping other people.

I fancied Gabby as soon as I saw her, and then when I spoke to her and realised how cool she was I was sold. I'd already sensed a bit of a vibe from her when she walked in and then I made my move by offering to help her do a pull up, so I wasn't that surprised when she picked me to go on a date. I had to cook her dinner and I didn't make her the best meal because I'm no Jamie Oliver, but she still fell for my charms.

Gabs had banter and she took the mickey out of me from the word go, which I loved. Obviously she looks stunning as well. She was the whole package and we just clicked. She's a bundle of joy and I feel like she makes me a better version of myself. She says I bring out the best in her too, so we definitely suit each other.

My journey didn't even start until Gabby entered the villa and we had the perfect ride. It got a bit rocky in parts (no pun intended), but we'd always get ourselves back on the same page and work it out because we liked each other so much. And some of the moments we spent together made me feel like life was perfect. You can't ask for much more than that.

Since I've left the villa, everyone keeps saying how proud of me they are. All my friends have said I really did them all proud, and strangers keep telling me what a gent I was. One woman clocked me at the airport the day I landed back from Majorca and her son, who was about six, turned around and started shaking when he saw me because he was so excited. I've even had middle-aged men giving me hugs.

Obviously I know how I am, but I didn't realise I'd touched so many people until I was back home. There was so much love for me and it

I still can't quite believe everything that happened on Love Island

shows that you should always be yourself. If you try and put on a show, it's never going to work. You'll get found out eventually. I could have tried to play it cool and acted like a proper lad and bantered non-stop, but that's not me. I was just being myself and it worked out for the best.

I still can't quite believe everything that happened on *Love Island*. On the first day I didn't know if I'd make it to the end of the week, so to be in the final was just amazing. I loved it so much I'd go back and do it all again tomorrow. Actually, can I?

Anyway, enough about me*, let's get on to my all-important relationship advice.

(*Don't worry about that we'll talk a lot about me in this bit as well.)

Dear Dr. Marcel

Dear Dr. Marcel,
is it okay to date
more than one
person at a time?

♥ ♥ ♡ ♥ ♥ ♡ ♥ ♥ ♡ ♥ ♥ ♡ ♥ ♥

If you're just having fun, yes, but not if you're into something proper. I think if you're upfront with someone and you're like, 'I'm single right now and I'm not really trying to get into anything long term', then you've been honest. But if you've made some kind of commitment, you can't then go and put it about.

I never try and play multiple girls but I did used to chat to a lot. You never know who's going to be right for you, innit? You could meet someone new when you've been talking to someone else, but you might feel like the new girl is more right for you. I'm all about keeping your options open until you find the right one.

The thing is, sometimes my mind wanders, sometimes my eyes wander and sometimes my body wanders. But I'm getting on in age now and I don't want to jump into a relationship where I'm not 100 per cent sure of it.

If something doesn't work out, you can spend several months waiting to see if it goes anywhere, and then you have to put yourself back into the game. I want something solid and real so I'd rather stay in the game until I meet the right person and say, 'I'm ready to do this now. Let's get on with it.' That's when you commit.

I know it was bad when I was with Gabby and I kissed those two other girls when me and all the boys were in Casa Amor, but I didn't have much of a choice. It was part of a game and it was all really light hearted. Gabby already knew about the first girl I'd kissed, but when she found out there was a second one she was so angry with me. It wasn't like I was keeping it from her on purpose. Neither kiss meant anything so I didn't feel like it was even worth mentioning.

Gabs had every right to feel annoyed and upset with me, and if I could go back and have my time again, I would have told her what had happened the minute I stepped back into the villa. Kissing someone else wasn't something I ever wanted to do in the first place, and by not telling her straight up it became a bigger deal. I was gutted she was upset and I would never want to hurt her, so I would definitely have played things differently.

Sometimes things just get a bit messed up. Look at what happened with Jonny and Camilla.

That was a complicated situation. Jonny came to me for advice because he wanted to get some feedback from someone outside of the situation and I could see what was going on so clearly.

I felt like there was chemistry between Camilla and Jonny but they both had their barriers up so it just wasn't happening. Nothing was flowing or clicking. Neither of them knew how the other one was feeling so they didn't want to be the one to let their guard down and put themselves out there. Sometimes you get a slow burner and if you're both holding back and panicking about what's going through the other person's head, you won't get anywhere. Sometimes it's not until one person makes a move it comes together.

Camilla was feeling insecure and she thought Jonny's head was going to be turned by Tyla. To be fair to the girl, she was right, but I do wonder if they could have taken their relationship further if there had been better communication between them.

There was definitely a spark between Tyla and Jonny, and as soon as she started putting it on him I knew it was game over for Cam because he clearly liked her.

I felt so bad for Camilla when Tyla and Jonny got together because it meant things were really awkward for her. In Jonny's defence, he was honest with Cam, but it's still not a nice feeling to be benched for someone else. But at the end of the day, did Jonny cheat? Not in my opinion.

Dear Dr. Marcel,
I want to finish with
someone but I really like
them as a person. Should
I drag it out for a bit
longer or bite the bullet
and dump them?

♡ ♡ ♡ ♡ ♡ ♡ ♡ ♡ ♡ ♡ ♡ ♡ ♡ ♡

I think the best thing to do if you're not into someone – whether you've been on a couple of dates or been dating for years – is to break up with them so they've got the chance to go off and meet someone else. Just because you don't want to be with someone doesn't mean there aren't plenty of other people who do. It's not okay for you to start laying it on other people just because you're not into the person you're with. Split up with them first.

What I'm saying, in a nutshell, is do the deed as soon as possible and don't double dip. Yeah, I know, I'm not one to talk if we're going on the past, but I'm not leading by example on this one. I'm just telling you how it should be.

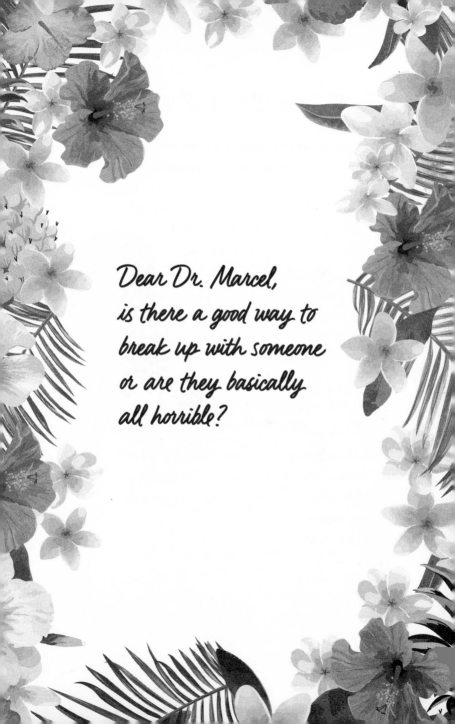

Dear Dr. Marcel,
is there a good way to
break up with someone
or are they basically
all horrible?

♡ ♡ ♡ ♡ ♡ ♡ ♡ ♡ ♡ ♡ ♡ ♡ ♡ ♡ ♡

It's always going to be difficult but honesty is the best policy. Communication is key. Here's the thing:

♡ You can't break up with someone over text because that's terrible.

♡ You can't break up with someone over the phone because that's not fair either. Also, they might seem like they accept it and then two months down the line they might say they think you need to meet up and do it face to face. You're leaving the door open for them to want to see you for a final goodbye. You want to close that door and lock it.

♡ Don't ghost someone because that's the worst thing you can do to a person. They'll be like, 'What did I do wrong?' At least have the balls to let them know.

The best thing you can do is meet with someone face to face. Have your reasons ready and explain them to them. If they try to argue with you, you've got to stand firm. If you're being totally straight and laying it on them and you've got good reasons, it doesn't leave them a lot of room for manoeuvre. It's much harder to fight reason than someone who's giving it the old 'I don't want to hurt you, but . . .'

I would also always recommend breaking up with someone in a public place or at their place so you can always leave. If you do it when they're round your house, it could end up being really hard to get them to leave. And if they're crying, it's horrible. It's not a good look to boot someone out when they're crying.

Dear Dr. Marcel,
is a slow fade an
acceptable way of
dumping someone?

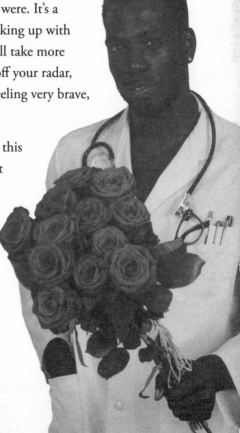

A slow fade is always fine if you're not in a serious relationship. But if you've been with someone for a long time, it's not okay.

If you've just been with someone a few weeks or months, you can start slowing down the communication and not being as available as you were. It's a longer way of breaking up with someone and it will take more time to get them off your radar, but if you're not feeling very brave, it's the way to go.

I've probably used this method in the past without realising it, but never with anyone I've been seeing properly. A proper relationship deserves a proper break-up.

Dear Dr. Marcel,
I'm still totally in love
with my ex but I know
it's game over. How can
I get over them?

♡ ♡ ♡ ♡ ♡ ♡ ♡ ♡ ♡ ♡ ♡ ♡ ♡ ♡ ♡

This is a tough one because I'm usually the one that breaks up with other people. I've been really lucky that I haven't been hurt that badly and I've been able to move on pretty quickly. I've ended every single relationship I've been in. Not that I've got commitment issues or anything, but I'm pretty good on picking up if things aren't working out. If I feel like things are going south, I take a step back and let it fizzle out (see above).

Despite having spent seven weeks with loads of other couples who were breaking up and making up constantly, I'm not one for my own relationship dramas. 'Cos of that, if I start arguing with a girl, I'll back off and let things come to a natural end.

With the last few relationships I've been in, we've both realised we weren't in the right headspace for anything serious, so we were honest with each other and went our separate ways. I wasn't left crying on the sofa or anything because I knew it was right.

Even with the girl I was with for seven years, we didn't break up as much as just kind of drift

We were pretty young and I think we both wanted to get out there and experience more

apart. Neither of us was feeling it any more and we knew it wasn't right, so there wasn't any big, dramatic ending to it. We were pretty young and I think we both wanted to get out there and experience more. Not just having sex with other people. But definitely that too.

Some people say that the best way to get over a relationship is to jump into another one, but it's not about that. Jumping into bed with someone isn't going to mend a broken heart. It'll just take your mind off it for a while.

If you've been in a relationship for a long time, the chances are you'll have been spending a lot of your time focusing on someone else. So take that time for yourself now and take really good care of yourself. You could start going to the gym or travel or do something you've always wanted to. Instead of making time for someone else, make time for you. There are so many things you can do to better yourself, and then when you get together with someone new you'll have your own stuff going on and it won't be all about them. You'll be doing it on your terms.

You need to get yourself into a good frame of mind after a break-up, so once you've found yourself and who you are again, then you can start looking for someone else. Don't rush into anything, and keep in mind that in a couple of years' time you probably won't give your ex a second thought.

Dear Dr. Marcel,
should you put all
your eggs in one
basket?

So this is carrying on from what I said above.
A relationship should be balanced and you can't
be piling your eggs into someone else's basket
and not keeping any eggs for yourself. I am all in
when I'm in a relationship, but I always keep at
least half a dozen eggs back so I don't lose myself.

When you're with someone you've still got to be
you for you. You've got to be yourself and stay
true and still do the things you enjoy doing on
your own. If you do that you won't be constantly
thinking ,'If this relationship ends, I'm done for.'

Some of my friends drop everyone out as soon
as they get a girlfriend, and they alienate people.
Or they stop going out to the gym and doing
things they love because they're all about the
other person. When you do that you're sacrificing
yourself and you will be left with nothing if
you split up. You'll have to start again and get
back in contact with all your mates you've pied
off. Shame.

There were couples in the villa who were literally
together all the time and didn't leave each other's
side. But Gabby and I had this kind of unsaid

agreement where we'd both do our own things in the daytime. If she wanted to sunbathe and I wanted to chill in the shade, that's what we did, and we didn't moan to each other about it. We'd go and work out or chill and have time to ourselves. Then we'd come back together and have a chat and a kiss, and then we'd go about our business again. We weren't glued to each other, which is healthier.

It was so easy for people to be on top of each other in the villa, and one of the things I always say about relationships is that you've both got to be able to be yourselves outside of the relationship. Do whatever you want to do when you're apart, and then when you're together, you're together.

Dear Dr. Marcel,
is it a good idea to
stay friends with
an ex?

I've never had a relationship where things have ended really badly and the girl has ended up hating me. I've always had friendly break-ups, so I guess I've always been on good terms/friends with my exes.

Of course, when you actually break up there is hurt involved, so there have been some angry feelings here and there, but usually within a month we're mates again. I think, again, part of that is because I'm such an upfront person. If I feel like things aren't going well, I will say it to someone, and that way there are no nasty surprises. I have respect for them and if I don't feel like we're going in the right direction, I'll say, 'I don't think it's working out for these reasons.' If you're saying how you really feel, it's hard for someone to be annoyed or irrational about it. There's no reason for someone to hate you if you're honest.

Do I go out with all my exes for dinner and hang out with them all the time? No. Do I think it's nice if you can stay mates with someone after a break-up? Yes. But not if there are still feelings involved. That's when it gets messy. If you still like the person or they still like you, keep your distance from each other until you're both over it.

Also bear in mind that if your ex gets with someone new, their new partner might not like you two being mates, so it could be that all communication has to come to an end. You need to respect that and let them move on.

Dear Dr. Marcel,
I hear what you're
saying but can men
and women ever really
just be friends?

Totally. Well, as long as you don't fancy each other, because that's a bit of a stumbling block.

I think it says a lot about a guy if he can be mates with a girl and not expect anything. It shows he's genuine and not just out for one thing.

I asked my best girl friend how she'd describe me to a girl if she was to try and set me up, and she said, 'Confident, generous and lovely.' I think that's a pretty good sales pitch.

Dear Dr. Marcel,
when does romance
become cheesy?

I think romance is an amazing thing, but there is a line, people. If you think of something romantic you'd like to do for someone and it even makes you feel a bit sick, don't do it. That advice is straight from the heart.

I've got to be honest; I have done some bare romantic things in my time. I can be a bit soppy when I'm in a relationship (especially after I've drunk red wine).

Before I went into the villa my most romantic moment ever had been when I met up with my ex for a chat about a month after we'd split up. I dropped her home and we were sitting in her car chatting and it was full-on raining outside. She got out and walked towards her house and I was all pumped up on romance so I dramatically jumped out of the car, ran over to her and kissed her in the rain like we were in a film.

I reckon by far the most romantic thing I did in the villa was when I went on my final date with Gabby. For anyone who didn't see it, I plotted this grand gesture for two days, and it involved me stealing a jar from the kitchen, a pencil and

a load of papers from cigarette boxes. I thought
of all the reasons I love Gabby and I got Camilla
to write them on the pieces of paper in her nice
handwriting. I put them all in the jar and got
Gabby to pick them out one by one while we were
having a picnic. I swear down, she loved it. She
cried and told me I'm amazing. She's not wrong.

Just in case you want to steal my idea, here's what
I wrote as inspo:

♡ I love your unique style and the vibrant
   clothes you wear.

♡ I love that when you kiss me you leave
   lipstick on my face.

♡ I love that you forgive me when I make a
   stupid mistake.

♡ I love it when you smile at me but don't say
   a word.

♡ I love that you're perfect but you do not have
   a clue.

♡ I love that I can be the man to say I've fallen
   in love with you.

I reckon I'm going to write a poetry book next.

Dear Dr. Marcel,
I always worry I like
people more than they
like me when I first
start seeing someone.
Should I play it cool?

The early bit of a relationship is always a bit like smoke and mirrors. You've got to style it out until you know what's going on. The moment you act like you're scared or worried about what the other person is thinking it makes them think they've got the upper hand.

When Gabby wanted to compete for a date with Mike along with the other girls I wasn't happy about it, but I had to hold my nerve and let her fly free. I'm not a controlling type at all but I could easily have said I didn't want her to do it. Instead I had to trust her. We already had a bond so I wasn't going to get all paranoid about it and worry about her running off with Mike. If she did, she did, and at least I would find out early on that it wasn't going to work out.

You can't force anything and you'll know if someone is into you or not. You just need to get through those initial stages and then you'll start to feel more secure. You can't start being all like, 'Do you like me?' when you've only been on two dates because it could well put someone off.

So in short: Be yourself, but play it a bit cool for the first few weeks.

Dear Dr. Marcel,
I know my mate's girlfriend is cheating on him with another dude. Should I tell him?

All day long. If I ever saw one of my brethren's girls with another guy, I would tell him straight away, no messing. I wouldn't want to see one of my mates get mugged off and even though it may be a bit of a case of 'don't shoot the messenger', if he's annoyed with you, it will only be temporary. It's the bro code and it has to be stuck to. I don't know what the female equivalent would be. Girl code sounds a bit boring. Lady laws? Anyway, stick by your sisters.

My mates are my priority. That's why I had to tell Dom when I heard the rumours about Mike and Jess getting it on outside of the villa. Dom was ready to commit to the girl and he risked his place in *Love Island* because of her, so it was right that he should know.

At the end of the day if you play games, you'll end up getting played yourself. No doubt.

Dear Dr. Marcel,
girls are always telling
me I'm too 'nice'!
Is there such a thing?

In one of my early relationships my girlfriend actually said to me, 'Marc, you're too nice.' But in my opinion you *can't* be too nice in a relationship. I know some people like to be a little bit 'treat 'em mean to keep 'em keen', but I don't think there's anything wrong with being courteous and gentlemanly. That's just how I am and it's not an act. You can tell if someone is nice off their own bat or if they're doing it just to win you over. It's pretty easy to tell the difference because they can't keep up the act for long.

Having said that, you don't want to be walked all over. If you're a naturally nice person and you want people to feel looked after, don't change that. But you should never let yourself be a doormat. You can't let people take advantage of you because there are a lot of people out there who would happily do that. You've got to protect yourself.

Gabby said she loved me being nice in the villa, but she also wanted the opportunity to do a bit more of the chasing because I probably seemed a bit 'all in' at times. But I'm not someone who backs off to keep a girl interested. It would have been weird if I'd suddenly started to act like I wasn't that bothered about her when I clearly was. I had no choice but to stay true to myself. At the end of the day, being genuine paid off for me.

Dear Dr. Marcel,
there's a girl I've liked for ages but she only goes out with guys with blonde hair who ride motorbikes. I've got dark hair and I drive a Nissan Micra so I'm definitely not her type on paper. Should I dye my hair and buy a motorbike so she notices me?

No, no. And no. You've always got to be yourself or the person you're trying to impress won't be falling for *you*. They'll be falling for the person you're pretending to be and things will soon start to crumble. You can dye your hair all the colours of the rainbow and walk down the street wearing head-to-toe leather but you'll still be the same person inside.

You can't change who you are for anyone. And if someone doesn't like you because of your appearance, all is not lost. Appearances don't mean anything. If you have the personality and charisma to woo someone even though you don't look like their fantasy man, that's what really counts.

If someone is superficial and they only care what you drive and what watch you wear, that is not the kind of person you should get with. One of the things I said to everyone in the villa is that it doesn't matter what your type is on paper because you have to fall in love with someone's personality first. You might look at someone and go, 'Oh my god, they're amazing', and then you talk to them and they're a drip and you get turned off in a second.

Kem was not Amber's type on paper but she fell in love with his personality and then fell head over heels in love with him.

I was looking for someone who has the same personality traits as me. I wanted someone chilled, laid back and wise. They had to like to party, but at the same time they needed to be creative and like to chill out a lot too. That's the kind of person I like to spend my time with on a day-to-day basis and that's nothing to do with what they look like and how they dress.

Don't be put off if you like a girl who's only ever gone out with tall, dark and handsome and you're short, pale and a bit questionable looking. If you've got a good personality, you should totally still make a play for someone. They might think you're so amazing and funny and clever they don't even mind that you drive a Nissan Micra. That's when you know you've got a keeper.

When I was in the band we met a lot of girls who loved us just because of who we were. When we went clubbing girls would hang around our table because we were in the VIP area. They saw that we were living the good life and they wanted a bit of it.

It was never about them getting to know us and then falling for us because we were a laugh. I got pretty good at spotting those types and I would go out of my way to avoid them. I would never have gone out with someone who liked me just because I was in the charts. I've always wanted someone to like me for me.

At the end of the day, looks are going to fade as you get older. If you go out with someone because they're good looking, but they're boring, one day they won't be as good looking and they'll *still* be boring, and you're stuck with that. Looks fade, personality grows.

Dear Dr. Marcel,
In your opinion what's
the key to a good
relationship?

Honesty and communication are everything. If you've got an open and honest relationship, you're more likely to go further and stay together. If you can talk to someone and be really honest with them, you're winning.

Even if you just need to tell someone that you don't like something or you wish they did a certain thing more often – if you can talk openly to someone they can take what you're saying on board and your relationship will develop. If they can't deal with your honesty, it's a sign that things might not work out long term. If people can't take honest criticism and discuss things without getting angry or offended, you're in a bit of trouble.

You do always have to think about the other person's feelings, but you shouldn't have to dumb yourself down because you're scared of offending them all the time. Don't bowl in and outright insult them, but if you feel strongly about something, you have to be able to express yourself without them taking it the wrong way.

If you're a strong person who speaks their mind and the other person doesn't like it, you're going to clash. You can't totally change your personality to make them happy because that will make *you* unhappy. Stay honest and stay true and you'll be on point.

Dear Dr. Marcel,
my mate's ex is bare
fit and she's been
flirting with me like
crazy. Is it okay for
me to date her?

No. I would never date one of my friend's exes. If it's just a girl they met on a night out and had a brief romance with, then maybe. But if they were properly together for a while, it's a no-go for me, and I would suggest it is for you too.

When Kem walked in and saw Chloe in the villa, he immediately recognised her as his mate's ex. Kem's mate and Chloe weren't ever going to get married or anything but Kem still didn't feel comfortable with being paired up with her. It wasn't what he wanted. I think because she was the only girl who stepped forward for him he felt like he had to try and make it work, but it wasn't what he would have chosen, and even though he didn't do anything wrong he still felt like a bit of a snake.

When you're young everyone dates each other and my mates and I went out with some of the same girls. But now? No way. Can you imagine? There's no way you wouldn't end up talking about your mate at some point and it would be horrible. Imagine if they'd been through a bad break-up too. It would make things so awkward with your mate, and you've got to respect them and put your friendship first.

Dear Dr. Marcel,
how do you know if
you're in love?

I've been in love twice. Maybe three times if puppy love counts. My first real love was with my girlfriend of seven years, and now the second time is with Gabby.

People might think I fell in love with Gabby pretty quickly but it's so intense in the villa. When you're on the island, every week feels like a month. Every emotion you have is magnified. You have so much downtime that even though Gabs and I did our own thing a lot, we ended up spending so much time together it was like our relationship was on fast forward all the time.

When I was in Casa Amor I was dying to get back and be with Gabs. I didn't want to be in there with all the new girls. I wanted to be in the villa with Gabby again because that's where I was happiest. Just being around her made me happy.

When I first saw Gabby again after that time away she looked amazing. I fell in love right at that moment. After that my feelings kept building and building, and now it's something else altogether.

Personally, I know when I'm in love when all I want to do is spend my time with that person, and I get this amazing feeling whenever I see them. When you're apart from that person all you do is think about what they're doing and when you can see them again. I love that.

Little things trigger your emotions here and there and you suddenly realise that even though you've only just seen them, you still want to drop them a message to see how they are. Then when you get a message back suddenly you're smiling without even realising it.

I find it so hard not to hug Gabby all the time when we're together. There are loads of little things she does that make me think, 'I love you'. It's all the little bits that add up. It's when you wake up and someone is the first thing you think about. That's when you know you're in love.

Dear Dr. Marcel,
I've been seeing this
guy but I caught him
liking some other girl's
selfies on Instagram.
What's up with that?

The way that the world is now you cannot do anything without it being picked up on. If you go somewhere and someone takes a photo, everyone knows where you are, and if you like someone's picture, everyone sees it. But it could have been totally innocent.

If you're seeing a girl and you like another girl's picture, or they like yours, it can look like something it isn't and lead to arguments. And you've got no control over who likes your posts. So don't jump to conclusions. At the end of the day, if someone is playing the field, you'll find out one way or another anyway, but don't be suspicious about every little thing they do on social media because you'll do your own head in.

Social media is both good and bad for dating. It's a good place to meet people, and if you fancy someone, you can start following them on Instagram or Snapchat and sending them direct messages. There are so many ways for people who like you to try and crack on to you, and vice versa. But you've also got to respect people's boundaries, and if they're not responsive, leave them alone.

Dear Dr. Marcel,
I fancy this bloke but I
hate the way he laughs
at things that aren't
funny. Shall I go out
with him and hope I can
train him out of it?

♥ ♥ ♡ ♥ ♥ ♡ ♥ ♥ ♡ ♥ ♥ ♡ ♥ ♥

You should never get together with someone hoping they'll change. You can't train someone to laugh at different things or have nicer toes. If you really like someone, those little things shouldn't matter. You should like everything about them from their greatest features to their flaws. And if you don't, you're probably with the wrong person.

Dear Dr. Marcel,
I've got a first date
coming up with a girl
I've liked for ages.
Where should I
take her?

Right, this is a pretty loaded question because of course you have to know where *not* to take her too.

If you're old enough to drink, for me the best place to go on a first date is for cocktails at a nice bar. It's perfect because you can have a drink, which naturally loosens people up, and the conversation will flow more easily. Also, you can talk through the cocktail menu and flirt a bit and try each other's drinks.

Activity dates are also really good. For example, there's a cool place called Swingers in Bank in London where you can go for drinks and play miniature golf. It's fun and memorable and you get to see a different side to people.

I always pay on the first date. In fact, I tend to pay on pretty much every date, but it's up to other guys what they want to do. I'm not saying you have to, but it is a nice thing to do.

Dates need different levels and you can't rush into things. If you pull out the big guns early on, there's nothing to look forward to and you'll have to keep upping the ante. Build things up slowly so you keep it exciting. There's nothing wrong with taking a girl on a spa date after a couple of months, but there's no rush. And if you pull out a spa date after you've been seeing each other for a little while, they'll think you're amazing because they won't be expecting it.

Gabs and I started off small with me cooking her that terrible meal, and we also had the hot tub date. Both were low key but really nice. Then in the end we had our helicopter date and life was *lit*. But if we'd gone in the helicopter first, all the other dates would have felt like a bit of a let-down afterwards.

One of the best dates I've ever been on was when I took a girl to see Ed Sheeran and I did the whole VIP box thing with loads of champagne. It was amazing but I would never, ever do something like that for a first date. That would be weird.

Another time I planned a whole weekend for an ex-girlfriend and we went for dinner at a Michelin-starred restaurant and then got a suite at the Sanderson Hotel in London. It was such a nice night, but again we were pretty far down the line by then.

When you're with the right person you'll want to do fun stuff with them

When you're with the right person you'll want to do fun stuff with them. You'll want to experience everything you can with them. You'll want to share special moments so you'll keep coming up with new ideas.

On the flip side, if you're going on a first date, under no circumstances should you:

♡ Go for dinner. Eating out on a first date is a massive mistake. You probably won't want to eat much because you're so nervous. Plus, you'll be talking loads so you won't get much of a chance to eat because no one wants to talk with their mouth full. Meals are more for second or third dates when you know each other a bit better. You can take someone to a nice classy restaurant and you'll look like you've got a little bit about you.

♡ Go to the cinema. It's a terrible idea. You can't talk to each other and if the film is rubbish, it automatically equals a bad date. You go to the cinema with someone you've been seeing for several months, not several days. I once took a girl to the cinema to see *Battleship* and it's such a horrible film I fell asleep halfway through. My date really liked it and that was a pretty good sign we weren't meant for each other. We didn't go on another date after that, funnily enough.

♡ Meet the parents. I mean, why would you? Seriously? If someone takes you to meet their parents on your first date, run like the wind. I know I met Gabby's family pretty early on but they were special circumstances, and the whole parent thing shouldn't really come into play until much later on.

♡ Cook for someone. Especially if you're a terrible cook like me. Thankfully Gabs forgave me for the awful meal I made her, but if, like me, you're not a whizz in the kitchen, it could be really embarrassing.

♡ Tell them you love them. It's the first date. What's wrong with you?

Dear Dr. Marcel,
I'm a bit of a disaster
with relationships.
Please tell me the most
common mistakes people
make so I can try and
avoid them?

Communication is so important and some people don't talk to each other enough. Quite often in the villa people would talk to *me* about their relationship issues and not the person they were having problems with. If they'd been open with them, they could have got things sorted out a lot quicker. I was always happy to listen and give advice, but at times they could easily have cut out the middle man.

If you're having a bad day or the person you're with is doing your head in, it's better to talk to them than get more and more wound up. That way you can resolve things quickly instead of letting them fester. If you stew on something, it often turns into something more than it needs to. Once things start to pile up it becomes a bigger deal, so the best thing to do is squash it early, and you can only do that by chatting openly about it.

It's also really important to give someone their space. You don't want your girlfriend or boyfriend to feel smothered. Again, I saw that in the villa. Some of the couples couldn't do anything without each other and they ended up getting on each other's nerves sometimes. If you're too on someone all the time, you could end up pushing them away and they might not want to spend any time with you at all. Everyone needs their own time to feel free and not have to think about their relationship.

Expecting too much is another relationship killer. If you want someone who looks like David Gandy and has the personality of Will Smith and you don't want to settle for anything less, you're always going to be disappointed, and that's not fair on anyone you date. They'll never live up to your expectations. Be realistic. No one's perfect so you may have to be a bit flexible. Like, I know I'm never actually going to go out with Julia Roberts. Not until she meets me and falls in love with me, anyway.

Dear Dr. Marcel,
I'm bang into this
guy but I feel like
I'm putting in a lot
of work and not
getting anywhere.
Am I in danger of
over-grafting?

If you've been putting in effort for ages and they're not giving you good signs, enough now. You've got to have a cut-off point.

If you meet someone and you get their number and you try and set up a date and you're not getting anywhere, you've got to be honest with yourself: they're not that interested. If after two weeks they're still not committing to meeting up, you're probably not going to go out on a date with that person.

If they give you specific reasons and explain themselves, like if they're going on holiday or their gran is having her hip replaced and they've got to go and look after her 18 cats, then fair enough. But if they're batting you off with rubbish excuses, then you won't be sharing cocktails any time soon I'm afraid.

I think two weeks is a legit time to wait. If a date isn't locked down by then, you've been grafting too long. That's a huge warning sign right there. You don't want to be the one who's grafting hardest, and if they're showing no signs of grafting at all their end, you've got to drop it out. Harsh, but true.

Dear Dr. Marcel,
I'm pretty sure I've been
ghosted. What are the
signs to look out for?

Is someone totally ignoring your messages? Have they blocked you from their social media? Do their mates look the other way when they see you in the street? Then I'm afraid, my friend, you have officially been ghosted. It doesn't feel good but you've got to respect the process because there's nothing you can do about it.

I've ghosted a few people in my time and I feel bad about it, but sometimes you need to disappear. You can meet someone on a night out who you think is amazing. Then you look at their social media and realise they're into cosplay and get a bit freaked out. Or you start texting or WhatsApping and you think to yourself, 'Yeah, you were nice on the night, but I don't see this going anywhere.' In those circumstances you've got to quit while you're ahead.

Ghosting is not a nice thing to do, but if you've tried being honest with them and they're not getting it, it could be the only way. You don't want to hurt people's feelings, but if you've dropped enough hints you're not up for anything and they're on your case, it could be

the kindest thing to do so they don't waste any more time.

I have been guilty of not replying to messages and hoping they take the hint. I've been in a situation where my blue ticks are popping off on WhatsApp so the other person knows you've read their message, and then they send you another one when you don't reply. You have to start deleting messages before you've read them to try and shake them off.

Sometimes they'll send you a message saying, 'I guess we're not talking to each other any more then?' It's just well awkward. I mean, do you reply to that message and say 'no' or are you just encouraging them even more?

I was ghosted by a girl I was seeing in 2009 and it did not feel good. We'd been friends for the longest time and we'd been out on some dates here and there, and then we got together properly. I was doing a Blazin' Squad reunion thing at the time and I had zero time to see her. I was straight with her and I said, 'Babes, I don't really have time to do this right now. I've got to go Japan for a while, so can we put it on hold until I get back?' I think she took it the wrong way and thought I was trying to

bench her so she stopped replying to my messages.
I was like, 'I can't believe this is happening. She's
actually ghosted me.' I liked the girl so I could
have kept trying to stay in touch with her, but in
the end I had to be like, 'Bruv, accept it.' It would
have been muggy to deny the ghosting.

Dear Dr. Marcel,
I split up with this girl six months ago and she seemed to accept we were over. Now she's made a comeback and she won't stop messaging me all the time. What's that all about?

♡ ❣ ♡ ❣ ❣ ♡ ❣ ❣ ♡ ❣ ❣ ♡ ❣ ❣

Ah, mate, she's a classic zombie. You think she's gone for good and then she starts trying to make contact again when you least expect it.

When I came out of the villa and turned my phone on I had the most insane amount of zombies on my WhatsApp. It was *crazy*. There were some girls I hadn't spoken to for, like, two years getting in touch. I had to send about a million of those 'Who is this?' texts to people because it had been so long since I'd spoken to them their numbers weren't even in the phone anymore.

If you haven't spoken to them for ages, there's probably a reason and you should never go back. You only ever stay in touch with people if you want to, and if you've cut them out before, you clearly didn't want them in your life then; you still don't now.

Dear Dr. Marcel,
when is the right time
to tell someone you
love them?

I don't think there is a 'right time'. It's not something you can put a time limit on or plan for. Like, you can't start seeing someone and then think, 'I'm gonna tell them I love them in five weeks' time.' You'll know when it's the right time.

When Gabby and I were having a chat on the roof terrace in the villa one day I told her she was perfect for me. Then before I knew it, I said I loved her. I hadn't planned to, honestly, it came out of nowhere, and it wasn't the first time I'd said it either. It just kept popping out. It was like I had no control over it. Gabs didn't say it back to me so I was a bit gutted. She also tried to tell me I didn't love her yet. I don't think she believed I did, but I genuinely was falling in love with her so I went with my heart.

When Gabs realised she loved me she told Camilla first so she could get some feedback. She was trying to work out how she was going to tell me, and obviously in the end she got the other girls to lie down on the grass and spell it out for me, which was amazing.

What people don't know is that she had already said it to me once before that night. It was when we were having a pool party one day, but it wasn't shown on TV. A song came on which had the lyrics 'If you love me say you love me', so I ran over to her, picked her up, spun her around and said, 'I love you.' She said, 'I love you too.' We didn't talk about it afterwards or anything but we both knew what it was.

It's honestly not the end of the world if you tell someone you love them and they don't say it back to you straight away. You've got that feeling inside of you and that may have to be enough for now. If you want to tell them you love them and it feels right (and it's not, like, two days after you first met), go for it. But you have to accept that they may not be ready to say the same to you just yet.

Sometimes two people are totally in sync and it's the right time for both of them to say it. But if you fall in love before the other person, don't be upset if they're not there with you yet. Everyone has different thresholds of love. You've got to be willing for them to take their time.

In my experience, once you feel the love for someone they will feel it from you anyway. Like,

It's honestly not the end of the world if you tell someone you love them and they don't say it back straight away

I've been doing loads of PAs in nightclubs recently and so many people have been coming up to me and saying, 'We love you, Marcel', and I've felt love back for them because they appreciate what I've got going on. If you feel love, it will pour out of you. It's not something you can hide.

I would never recommend throwing 'I love you' about like it doesn't mean anything just because you think it's what the other person wants to hear. Those three words are a big deal. I'm quite a romantic soul and I am open and I like to express my feelings, but I would only ever say, 'I love you' if I really meant it.

Dear Dr. Marcel,
girls keep laughing
at my chat-up lines.
Where am I going
wrong?

You're going wrong using chat-up lines in the first place, bruv. It's not 1985 you know. I've got five rules when it comes to chat-up lines, and I'm going to share them with you.

1) Never use chat-up lines.

2) The best way to get a girl's attention is to make eye contact and get a vibe via the eyes.

3) Smile, because you'll come across as open and friendly and you'll look much more approachable. Whenever I smile at a girl they get a bit giggly, so it clearly works.

4) If you're at a bar, offer to buy a girl a drink.

5) Don't use chat-up lines.

Chat-up lines are unnecessary and guys try to use them as banter, but it does not work. If a girl gives me eye contact and her eye contact game is strong, I already know she's interested so I don't need to lay any cheesy lines on her. If I'm in a bar or a club and a girl's given me the eye, I know about it. It's even happened to me in a shop, and when that happens you get a vibe and you know they want to talk to you.

I could never go up to a girl and throw down a line like, 'Hey, darlin', are your feet hurting? Because you've been running through my mind all night.' That kind of behaviour is not acceptable. Why would anyone do it? It's so cringey.

I would rather be confident and walk up to a girl and say, 'Hi, what's going on?' and give her a nice compliment. Like, tell them they've got nice eyes or that you like what they're wearing. That shows that you're obviously attracted to them and you've noticed what they've got going on. The kind of line I would use is: 'You look amazing. Can I buy you a drink?' Boom. That will get the conversation flowing.

Probably the craziest place I've met someone and ended up going on a date was when I was walking down Carnaby Street in London. This girl was working in a shop and she gave me the eye as I walked past. Then when I walked back towards my office she stepped out of the shop and I gave her my business card. She gave me a call later and it went from there. You can meet people anywhere as long as you can read vibes and give vibes.

I've always had a big smile.

The Mighty Ducks were cool back then, honest.

With my older sister.
She's always kept me
on track.

Aged 2 with my
mum. Loving that
shirt!

Showing off my moves aged 8.

Looking smart aged 4.

I've got my serious face on here.

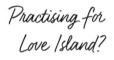

*One glove, no top.
Now that's style.*

*Practising for
Love Island?*

*With my Blazin' Squad
boys back in the day.*

© DMC / Contributor

Gabs and I had literally just arrived back in the UK from Majorca.

I think my smile says it all!

© DMC / Contributor

This is just a
normal day for me
(but not at all).

Anyone for
champagne?

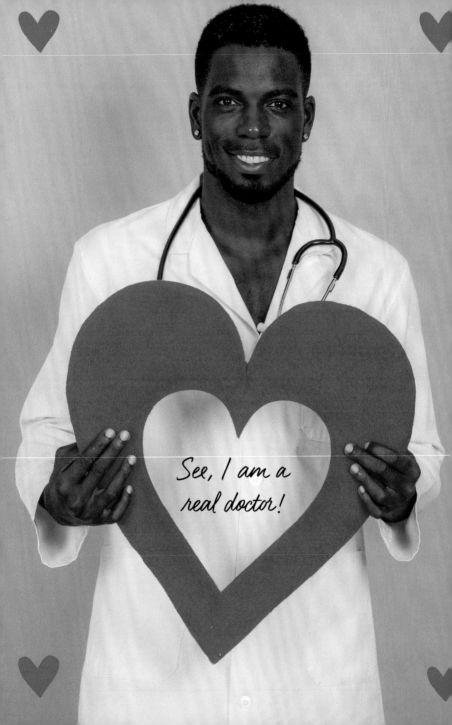

Dear Dr. Marcel,

I'm pretty sure I'm being pied off by this guy but he's totally breadcrumbing me and I keep falling for it. I'm 99 per cent sure he's got no intention of actually going out with me but he's hooked me in with his banter so every now and again I think there could be a chance for us. Is there?

There isn't. Sorry, babes, I'm just saying it like it is. I breadcrumbed a few girls in my younger days because I can be quite flirty and I probably gave the wrong impression. I'd message girls about going on a date, and then the day before – if I wasn't feeling it – I'd make my excuses. I did have every intention of going on a date, honest, but then I'd change my mind.

I never set out to lead anyone on and sometimes you do genuinely like a girl you're talking to. Then you meet someone else you like more so you back off, and it looks like you've been stringing them along.

Some people just like getting attention from lots of different people at the same time, and if someone's messaging you but nothing solid is coming from it – they're leading you on. And you're probably not the only one.

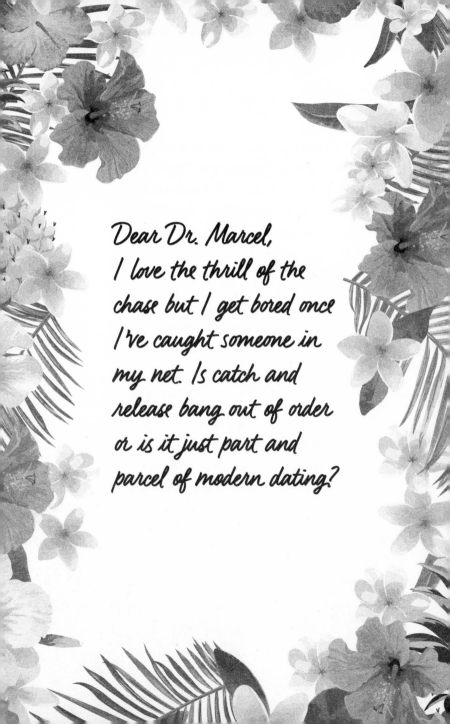

Dear Dr. Marcel,
I love the thrill of the
chase but I get bored once
I've caught someone in
my net. Is catch and
release bang out of order
or is it just part and
parcel of modern dating?

I do not agree with catch and release at all. It's people's feelings you're playing with. Sometimes I do kind of like the chase myself, but I would never chase someone to see if I could get them just for the ego boost, and neither should you.

It's horrible if you pursue someone and make them think you like them, and then once you reel them in you lose interest. You may think it's a bit of fun but they won't see it like that.

Catch and release doesn't make sense to me. The fun part of a relationship is really getting to know someone. There were some people in the villa who were trying to crack on with anyone they could and you could tell they enjoyed all the attention, but I was always going to wait for someone I had a connection with to come through the door.

I wanted to find someone to build something with, whereas other guys just wanted to boost their self-esteem. I think the final showed which people really wanted to meet someone they could stay with long term and which ones didn't.

The fun part of a
relationship is really
getting to know
someone

Dear Dr. Marcel,
I tried to lay it on this hot girl last week and I didn't realise her boyfriend was standing right next to her. It was so embarrassing and I'm still not over it. Please tell me I'm not the only one who has pulling fails?

♡ ♡ ♡ ♡ ♡ ♡ ♡ ♡ ♡ ♡ ♡ ♡ ♡

Geez, it happens to the best of us. I've crashed
and burned in my time but you have to dust
yourself off and crack on.

This one time me and my boys were out at our
favourite club in Woodfordis North east London.
I saw this bare fit girl and it was quite late by that
point so I'd had a few drinks. I went over and
started dancing near her but as I jumped into a
move my legs went from underneath me and I fell
flat on my arse. My buddies started laughing and
the girl I was trying to impress had to help me up
off the ground.

For one of the only times in my life I was totally
speechless and I walked away and hid at our table.
The girl came and found me later on and we had
a chat and exchanged numbers, but we didn't
end up going on a date or anything. I think the
damage had been done.

Dear Dr. Marcel,
HELP! I was seeing this great guy for fun times with no strings and I've caught feelings. What the hell should I do?

♡ ♡ ♡ ♡ ♡ ♡ ♡ ♡ ♡ ♡ ♡ ♡ ♡ ♡

Don't panic, it's very easily done. Sometimes it happens without you noticing and by the time you realise, it's too late. But you can't fight it. If you catch feelings, it's just the way it is.

If the other person hasn't caught feelings as well, my advice is to keep quiet about it. If you start pouring your heart out to them when they think you're keeping things casual and they don't feel the same, you're going to feel rubbish about yourself. You need to keep how you're feeling to yourself and hope they end up feeling the same way. They may just be a few steps behind you and not ready to admit their feelings to themselves yet. If you still feel the same a month or two later and they're not giving you any strong signals they're on the same page, there's a strong possibility they may never be.

Catching feelings when you're not expecting it can be scary but it's life, and it's a part of relationships. Sometimes you catch feelings of anger and you end up hating someone, and sometimes you catch feelings of affection and you end up loving someone. We can't control that stuff. Sometimes our emotions are stronger than we are.

If you feel love building for someone, go with it, but keep yourself protected too. If you feel like things are starting to get out of control and the person you're in love with is never going to feel the same way, you've got to pull back or you'll end up getting really hurt. The deeper you get into something, the harder it's going to be to get yourself back out again.

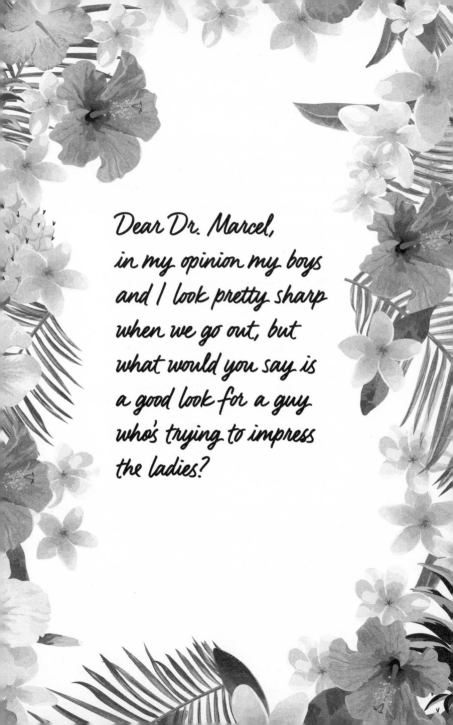

Dear Dr. Marcel,
in my opinion my boys
and I look pretty sharp
when we go out, but
what would you say is
a good look for a guy
who's trying to impress
the ladies?

Your clothes need to be a representation of you, innit. Like, I wear black quite a lot. Not because I'm a vampire but because I think it suits me and it looks good. You've got to be comfortable in what you're wearing, whatever it is.

I can't really tell you specific clothes you should wear in order to pull because everyone's dress style is different. But I will say that if you don't feel confident in what you're wearing, it will show a mile off. If you're wearing something that is outside of your comfort zone and you don't feel right, nothing else will be right. If you don't feel confident in yourself, you're not going to be confident enough to try and pull a girl. Unless you're really, really drunk, and that's not a good look either.

Even if you think your mate always looks cool, don't try and steal his style. What looks good on them may not look good on you. Some guys can put on a yellow and pink striped shirt and look the business, whereas someone else might not be able to pull off such a strong look. Go with what works for you.

I always like to have a nice watch on when I go out so I can give a girl the time if she asks, and other than that I'm casual but smart. I like a good pair of fitted jeans, a nice top and a decent pair of shoes or trainers that are clean and pristine. Girls like guys who look like they look after themselves and shoes say so much about a person. If you're wearing a pair of dirty, scruffy, beat-down trainers, you won't be giving out a good impression.

You should always be well groomed, and I can give you one amazing pulling tip for men: if your aftershave game is strong, you're more likely to get noticed. I wear Creed Aventus and I'm always being told I smell amazing by strangers. Honestly, it's an amazing scent and it makes you irresistible. It's the best smell in the world. The other aftershave I wear is Guerlain for men and that's also a big hit.

A good haircut is very important. Whenever I got a new haircut in the villa I felt like a new man. It gives you another level of confidence, so if you're going out, maybe get a fresh trim.

If you've got a fresh trim, nice garms and you smell good, you'll be looking fresh. You'll be

If you're wearing a pair of dirty, scruffy, beat-down trainers you won't be giving out a good impression.

stepping out big and you'll be out on the prowl smashing it.

As for what girls should wear? I'm no expert but again, go with what you feel good in. Gabs wore some really vibrant stuff in the villa and I loved her uniqueness. I found that so attractive. Just be you. You don't need to make yourself look like someone else or go over the top to stand out in a crowd.

I guess it's a good idea to leave a little bit to the imagination. Believe it or not it is possible to show too much. It's never good to have too much skin on show.

If you've got your legs out, maybe don't get your boobs out. And if you've got your boobs out, maybe wear something a little bit longer. If you look good, guys are going to check you out whether you're showing everything off or not. And there's something nice about a bit of mystery.

Dear Dr. Marcel,
what should I always
have in my snack pack
when I go out?

♡ ♡ ♡ ♡ ♡ ♡ ♡ ♡ ♡ ♡ ♡ ♡ ♡ ♡

I'm not a big user of snack packs. I think it's crazy that people go for a night out carrying a toothbrush just in case they pull. It must be weird if you get searched on the way into a club. The doormen will be like, 'What's this?' and you'll be like, 'Oh, it's just my foldaway toothbrush.'

I do carry condoms because I want to be safe, and also chewing gum because you can bang one in if you need to sort out morning breath.

What I'd really like is a tiny bottle of Creed so I could spray it on in the morning so the girl would be like, 'Wow, he still smells so great.' How cool would that be?

Dear Dr. Marcel,

I went on an amazing date but now I don't know how long to leave it until I get in touch. I'd definitely like to go for round two but I don't know if I should make the first move.

If the first date goes really well, the chances are you'll be in touch later the same night. That's assuming you're not already back at their place (see below for my advice about sex on first dates).

If a date's gone well there have been times when I've messaged a girl as soon as I've got home to say thank you for a nice night. I like to follow up a date to see if the girl had a good time or not because I think that's polite, but that's just me.

If it's gone *really* well, sometimes you can end up organising the next date the same night. To be fair, most of my dates go really well so that's not uncommon.

If you haven't heard from someone and you don't want to look too eager, wait until the following evening to message them. The likelihood is they're probably waiting for you to make the first move so it's a bit like a game of cat and mouse.

There's no rule that says it has to be the guy or girl that gets in touch first. Just go with the flow. If you want to drop someone a message, don't hold back. If you do that, things could fizzle out because you're both trying to play it cool, and that would be a waste.

If a date hasn't gone to plan, you want to pace yourself, so give it at least two days until you get in touch at the very minimum. You don't want to give the impression you're mad keen. Hopefully they'll have picked up the same vibe as you. That makes things easier all round.

Dear Dr. Marcel,
should you throw caution
to the wind and have sex
on a first date, or hold
back until later on down
the line?

♡ ♡ ♡ ♡ ♡ ♡ ♡ ♡ ♡ ♡ ♡ ♡ ♡ ♡

Unless things get really frisky and freaky I wouldn't suggest having sex on a first date. Have fun and have a nice little kiss or whatever, but hold back from putting out until at least . . . the second date? Nah, I'm only joking. You want to take your time.

You can tell what kind of relationship you're going to have with someone by how the first date goes. If the other person is bare flirty and they clearly want something to happen and they're not letting up, it's pretty hard to say, 'I think we should wait.' In that scenario it might progress to a physical thing pretty quickly.

But if you like someone and you do want it to go somewhere long term, you've got to stay strong, be honest and say, 'I don't want it to just be about sex.'

In all honesty, you need to have both kinds of relationships in your lifetime – ones that are purely physical and ones where you have more of a connection – so you can experience everything. Sometimes on a first date it's all about pure lust and in that moment you want to jump into bed with someone and you're happy to go with the flow. If you're both happy for it to just be about the physical, get your coat and get a taxi back to theirs, no question.

Personally, I never try to get into someone's pants on a first date. I'd rather be patient and let things happen when they're ready to happen. But sometimes it happens by accident.

You may get a vibe straight off that you want someone to be your girlfriend. But then you might be thinking, 'We haven't got a lot in common and this isn't going anywhere long term, but why don't we have fun for a while and see how it goes?'

Sometimes something more does end up developing, but if you have sex on a first date, you always run the risk that it could end up being a one-night stand. Some people have an attitude like, 'I'm not hugely bothered about seeing you again now we've done the deed.' I guess there's nothing for the other person to graft for. I know it's bad because they've done exactly the same thing as you, but they may not have as much respect for you if you sleep with them straight away. Or they may assume you're only after a bit of fun.

You'll soon know if someone thinks you're a
one-night stand because you probably won't hear
from them again, but it can go one of two ways.
Sometimes you'll wake up next to someone and
think, 'I want to give that person a cuddle' and
sometimes you'll be like, 'I need to get out of
here pronto.'

The majority of the time if you're not feeling the
vibe, you'll be the first one to wake up and you'll
be lying there thinking, 'Where am I? And can
I get away with leaving before the other person
wakes up?' Not that I would ever actually do that
because it's bang out of order.

You'll know by the way you feel the following
morning whether you're into someone or not.
If you're willing to try and escape through the
window to get away from them, this is probably
not someone you want to marry. But if you go
and get breakfast and chill out, it's obviously a
sign that there could be something more to it.

What you must never do is promise someone
the world to get into their pants and then never
contact them again. That is bad. A one-night
stand is only acceptable if you're both on the same
page and you're going to enjoy it for what it is.

If you take someone out on a date and feed them the gab just so you'll get some that night, it's wrong. You can't be leading someone on just so you can get freaky.

I haven't had a one-night stand since I was about 24 or 25 but I remember waking up with a hangover in my younger days thinking, 'What have I done? I need to get a cab home but I have no clue where I am.'

Now I'm older, I've calmed down a lot and I do think I want to find 'the one'. That's probably not going to happen if I wake up in a cold sweat miles away from home with a girl whose name I don't remember.

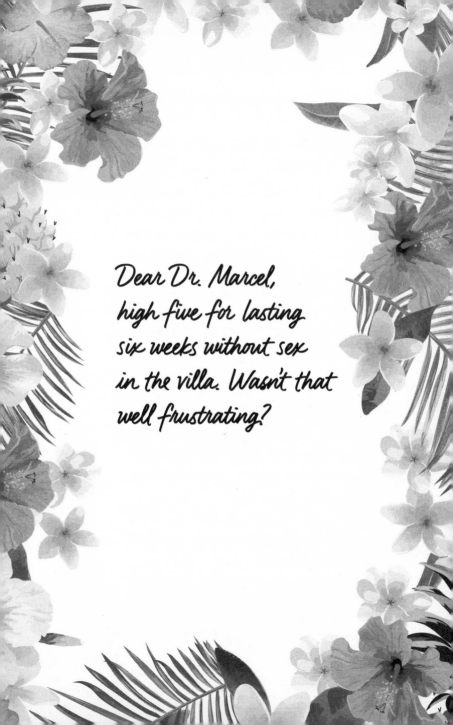

Dear Dr. Marcel,
high five for lasting
six weeks without sex
in the villa. Wasn't that
well frustrating?

♡ ♡ ♡ ♡ ♡ ♡ ♡ ♡ ♡ ♡ ♡ ♡ ♡ ♡

I think you could tell by how I was in the villa that I'm not all about the sex. I knew Gabby didn't want to do it on TV and I 100 per cent respected that so we didn't do anything. Was I gagging? Yes. Did I mind? Not in the least. I've had a lot of sex in my life and it wasn't like I was waiting to lose my virginity or something. I'm not a hormonal 16-year-old boy anymore.

Gabby also wanted to take things slow, because she had some fears, and I wanted her to feel comfortable at all times. I didn't want to do anything for the sake of it. Because sex wasn't getting in the way we had a chance to build a relationship. I was like, 'I don't mind at all because this girl is *amazing*.' I was happy to wait it out and make sure it was right. You need to build a relationship first so you've got the foundations anyway, and we had all those weeks to do that so it worked out perfectly. And now it feels like we're rock solid.

Me and Gabby made a pact that as soon as we got out of the villa we'd have sex and the wait was fun because we knew we had something to look forward to. And at the end of the day, as some of my mates pointed out to me, if we'd done it in the villa, that's a sex tape right there, and it's out there forever.

It's good to be patient and be a gentleman. If you're willing to wait, it shows you've got morals. You should never, ever pressure someone else into doing anything they don't want to do. And it's not about what the people around you are doing either. You've got to follow your own path.

I knew Gabby and I would have sex when the time was right, and when we did it was definitely worth the wait.

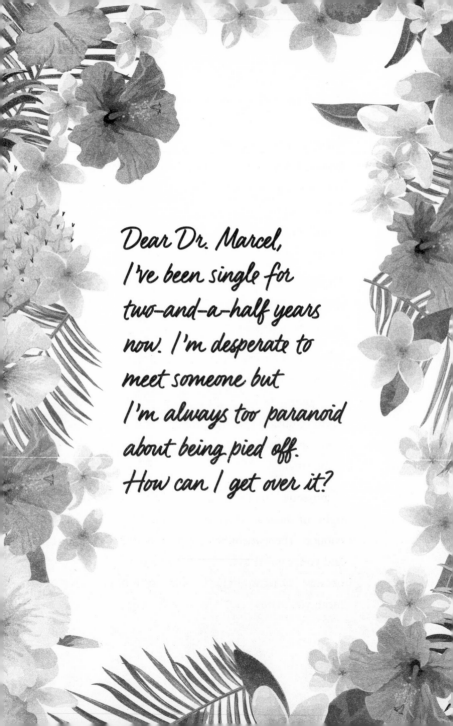

Dear Dr. Marcel,
I've been single for
two-and-a-half years
now. I'm desperate to
meet someone but
I'm always too paranoid
about being pied off.
How can I get over it?

Mate, you've just got to go for it. As everyone knows, I dealt with the biggest rejection in the villa when no one stepped forward for me when I first went in. I was pied so badly but I stayed confident in my abilities and my personality and I knew that someone would like me.

I don't know anyone who hasn't had to deal with rejection at some point. If you don't try, you'll never know what's out there for you.

What's going to happen if someone turns you down? Is the world going to stop turning? No. You might just feel a bit rubbish for a few minutes but it's better to go through that than feel crap every day because you're unhappy about being single.

If someone blows you out, it's because you're not right for them and not because you're not good enough. There are billions of people in the world and you're going to be right for one of them. Just because you're not right for one person it doesn't mean you're not perfect for someone else.

Dear Dr. Marcel,
how will I know if
someone is into me
when we're on a date?

You will soon know if a date isn't going well by the vibes. If you're sitting having your cocktails, at the beginning of the date there will naturally be a bit of a space between you. Then as the date goes on, you'll be able to pick up from the person's body language that they're opening up to you.

You might start touching each other's hands, and if you've already had a couple of drinks, there may be a bit of cheeky leg stroking going on. Me and Gabs stroke each other a lot. Some people might think that's a bit weird.

If someone starts leaning in and getting closer to you during the date, they're definitely into you, and you'll pick up on whether you should go in for a kiss or not. You can read that from their eye contact and how flirty they're being. I can look in someone's eyes and know they're saying to me, 'Boom, I really want to kiss you right now.' If you're giving each other the same eyes, you're both in the same place. But choose your moment wisely. You don't want to go in for a kiss and get a pie to the face.

Dear Dr. Marcel,
I've got a date next week
but I'm not sure if I like
the guy. Is there a good
way of ducking out early
if I'm not feeling it?

♥ ♥ ♡ ♥ ♥ ♡ ♥ ♥ ♡ ♥ ♥ ♡ ♥ ♥

Even if I'm not feeling a date, I will always do my best to be entertaining and polite. I would never, like, chuck some money on the table and say my goodbyes because that's so disrespectful. Stay for as long as you can without feeling uncomfortable.

If you're out for drinks, I reckon it's acceptable to leave after the third drink and say something like, 'I can't get too rowdy tonight because I've got to be up in the morning.' Then politely slip away.

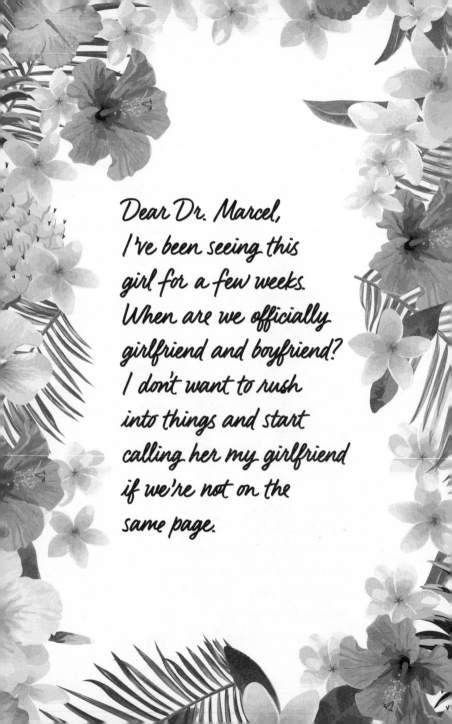

Dear Dr. Marcel,
I've been seeing this
girl for a few weeks.
When are we officially
girlfriend and boyfriend?
I don't want to rush
into things and start
calling her my girlfriend
if we're not on the
same page.

I think it needs to happen naturally. If you try to have a conversation about making things official and someone isn't feeling it, it makes things awkward. Things automatically progress when you want to spend all your time with that person and they want to spend all their time with you. When it comes to the point where you get to the weekend and you know you'll be spending it with each other, it's going the right way. Then you'll start seeing each other during the week, and before you know it you'll be with each other all the time.

When you know for certain that you're not going to meet someone else who would make you leave that person, you've become official. That's a big sign that you're actually in a relationship.

Sometimes people like to be told where they stand but I think if at any point you pressure someone into having a relationship and they don't feel like they're there, having that conversation can ruin things. If you let things go with the flow, you're more likely to end up on the same page at some point, so be patient.

If you let things go
with the flow, you're more
likely to end up on the
same page

Once you get into a routine with someone, you naturally turn into boyfriend and girlfriend. It might be that you overhear someone referring to you as their girlfriend or boyfriend and then you're like, 'Okay, it's official now.' But you don't always need to sit down and have 'the chat'.

Gabs and I did and we became girlfriend and boyfriend after three weeks, which is quick. But like I've already said, that's because everything was so magnified in the villa. It might have taken us a few months to get to that place on the outside, but in there it already felt like we'd been together a lifetime.

There have been times in the past when a girl has called me her boyfriend and it was a bit shocking. I was like, 'Oh, I didn't realise we were there yet', but I've secretly liked it. And anyway, even if they're not calling you their boyfriend or girlfriend to your face, the chances are they're already calling you that to their mates if you've been seeing each other for a while.

I think there were times when Gabby thought I was rushing things with the whole girlfriend thing. When I asked her to be my girlfriend she wasn't expecting it and for once she was lost for words. Then we sat down for a chat and by the end of the conversation I officially had a girlfriend.

Dear Dr. Marcel,
I've been out with this chick on a few dates and it's going well, but now she wants me to meet her mates. I feel like it's a bit too soon, but is there a 'right time' to do it?

♡ ♡ ♡ ♡ ♡ ♡ ♡ ♡ ♡ ♡ ♡ ♡ ♡ ♡ ♡

I think you can start meeting mates in, like, the second month. But you should do it in a way where you don't feel like you're on show. You don't want to go round to your girlfriend's house and find her friends sitting on the sofa holding question cards so they can grill you. Nah, mate. You don't want to be interrogated.

It's fine to meet her mates but take the pressure off by meeting them when you're with your mates too. If she's with her girl pals out at a bar and you're with your boys, at least you can mingle and it takes a lot of the pressure off. If you have a few drinks and a laugh in a group scenario, you won't feel like you're being thrown into the lion's den. It's important to make it a relaxed environment.

Of course I met Gabs' mum and brother in the villa very early on and that would never usually happen until much later on down the line in the real world. Whenever you meet your other half's family you're going to be a bit like, 'Really? Meeting the parents?' But at least you usually have time to build yourself up for it. In the villa it was like, 'Bam, here's the fam!'

There's no point in trying to impress someone's friends and family. The only thing you can do is be yourself. It is scary because you really want them to like you, but you can't put on a big show because it will come across as fake. The parents will know their son or daughter has picked you because they see something in you they like, so you're already one step ahead of the game. And hopefully the parents will see and like those things too.

I know it makes a difference what someone's friends and family think about you because it can have a big influence, but there's no point in stressing. At the end of the day, if they like you, they like you, and if they don't, they don't.

I've literally never been in a situation where parents don't like me. Everyone's parents always love me. It's really weird. I think it's because I'm friendly and approachable so they warm up to me. I don't try and get them on side, it just happens. If you have manners and you're polite, parents will love you whatever.

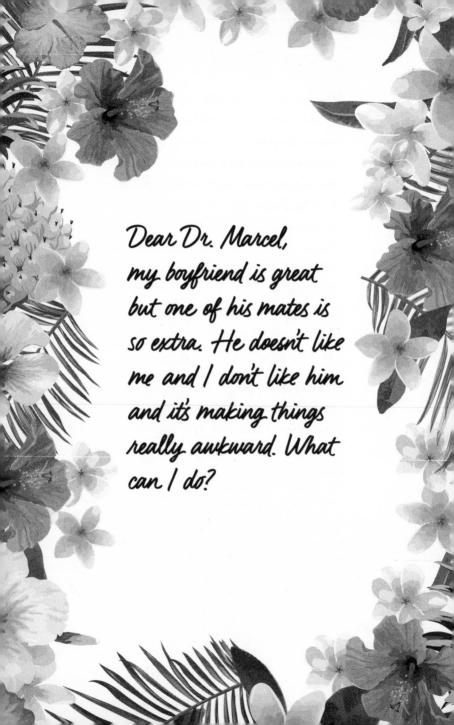

Dear Dr. Marcel,
my boyfriend is great
but one of his mates is
so extra. He doesn't like
me and I don't like him
and it's making things
really awkward. What
can I do?

If you're in a relationship with someone and one of their mates doesn't like you for whatever reason, keep in mind that everyone is entitled to their opinion and not everyone loves everyone else in this world. Don't make a big deal out of it. If the person still wants to be with you even if their mate is whispering in their ear, it's irrelevant. You're not in a relationship with their mate and all you can do is keep being the person your boyfriend or girlfriend loves. Even if that mate keeps trying to put you down or whatever, let them get on with it. Rise above it and they're the one who will end up looking like a fool.

If someone decides they want to break up just because one of their mates doesn't like you, do you really want to be with someone that spineless anyway? Nah. You want someone who always backs you and is willing to fight your corner.

Dear Dr. Marcel,

I'm well in love with my girlfriend and things have been wicked. Then the other day we had our first argument and it made me take a step back and wonder if we're right for each other after all. I don't want to get all dramatic about it but we said some pretty awful things to each other. Can we get past this?

♡ ♡ ♡ ♡ ♡ ♡ ♡ ♡ ♡ ♡ ♡ ♡ ♡ ♡

If you can't, bruv, your relationship is screwed. You can't let one argument dictate whether or not you're supposed to be with someone. All couples argue. Look at Liv and Chris in the villa. They had some blazing rows but they always worked it out, and if anything it made them stronger.

You need to deal with arguments head on. You both need to have your say but one of you needs to try and remain calm if you're going to work things out. If someone is screaming and shouting at you, don't scream and shout back because you won't get anywhere. Things will only escalate and become more heated.

Try talking to them instead. If you talk to someone calmly, hopefully they'll calm down. But if it gets to the point where they're not listening to you, take some time out. Say something like, 'I'm going to go and do my thing and you can go and do yours, and when we've both calmed down we can talk, innit.'

You're never going to sort it out if someone is irate so give them their space and wait until they're ready to talk. Even if they need a day to process things and then they want to chat about it. It's much better than trying to sort it out when emotions are running high.

Gabs and I had our moments on the island. She was annoyed about something I did one day and we had some cross words. Then I said something like, 'Oh is this the start of it all?' because I was feeling a bit rubbish about it. It was a throwaway comment but it wound her right up and it turned into something bigger. At that point it's best to step away.

As for saying horrible things to each other during an argument? It's probably going to happen. Words fly out without you meaning them to, and to a certain extent you've got to give each other a 'get out of jail free' card and know that if something was said in the heat of the moment, they probably didn't mean it. If there's a particular thing that's upset you, talk it out. Don't sit on it and feel angry inside. You'll carry that around with you and get more and more wound up and it'll end up coming out at some point anyway.

It can be hard to get past something that has really hurt you. In that situation you need to let

It can be hard to get past something that has really hurt you

the other person know why it's made you feel so crap and hope they apologise.

If someone says something really, *really* awful that makes you properly emotional, you have to think about whether you want to be with a person who can treat you so badly. It could be a sign that there's more of that to come further on down the line.

If you don't think you can ever get over something someone's said to you, there's probably no coming back from it. You can tell yourself you've forgiven them but it will always be in the back of your mind, so at some point you'll have to drop them out.

Dear Dr. Marcel,
who should apologise
first after an
argument?

♡ ♡ ♡ ♡ ♡ ♡ ♡ ♡ ♡ ♡ ♡ ♡ ♡ ♡

It's not always about who is in the wrong or who caused the argument. Do you know what? Sometimes I just suck it up and apologise even when I feel like the other person is to blame. Sometimes you've got to be the bigger person.

There was a moment in the villa when I was talking to Gabs and she had to go and run to speak to one of the producers about getting the girls to do the 'I love you' message for me. I was in the middle of saying something to her and I got annoyed because she just went off. I was like, 'Babes, are you really going to walk away halfway through my conversation?' Obviously I didn't know it was because she had to go somewhere, and she couldn't explain the circumstances to me either because it was a secret.

I'm not even sure the argument was *actually* about Gabs walking off and me getting annoyed. I think there had been a bit of a build-up and a few things had happened here and there, and then it kind of blew up.

We both went to bed angry that night but then the next morning we spoke about it. She couldn't see my point of view and didn't understand why I'd got upset, so I explained my reasons and said she'd been rude. We went back and forth but in the end she got it. I saw things from her point of view too, so we got over it. She apologised for walking off and I apologised for overreacting.

You need to empathise with the other person's feelings and realise that their interpretation of an argument might be very different to yours. Both of you need to get your points across and you need to really listen to the other person if you want to get it sorted. Sometimes the other person just wants to know that their points have been heard.

Rows did kick off in the villa quite a few times, and even though I don't like getting involved in other people's arguments because it can escalate them, when Montana and Olivia had a big row (ironically about Liv being confrontational with Sam) I felt Liv was in the wrong on this ocassion. I will stick up for someone if I think the other person is in the wrong all day long. I stepped in to try and help and Liv got annoyed with me when I was just trying to sort stuff out. Liv and I ended up arguing too and I was well confused.

I was annoyed that Liv let rip and shouted at me, but tensions were running high and I had to take a step back and realise it wasn't personal. Anyone who had got in the middle of them would have got an earful.

Liv and I kissed and made up in the end and it was all fine. I didn't hold a grudge. If you argue, whether it's with a friend or someone you're seeing, you've got to get over it and crack on and hope the other person does the same thing. I wanted to have a nice time in the villa so I accepted her apology and moved on. At the end of the day it was supposed to be Love Island, not Argument Island.

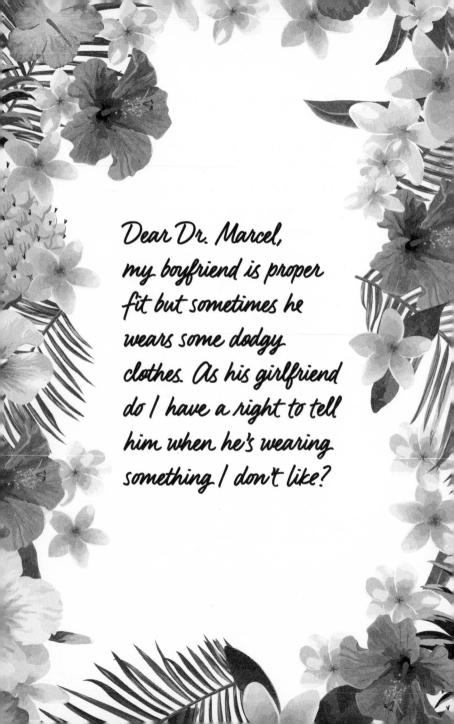

Dear Dr. Marcel,
my boyfriend is proper
fit but sometimes he
wears some dodgy
clothes. As his girlfriend
do I have a right to tell
him when he's wearing
something I don't like?

♡ ♡ ♡ ♡ ♡ ♡ ♡ ♡ ♡ ♡ ♡ ♡ ♡ ♡

Do you know what, you should never, ever, ever, ever tell someone they look bad. If you don't like what they're wearing but they do, that's all that counts. It's not you wearing it and if he feels confident in his garb, let him get on with it.

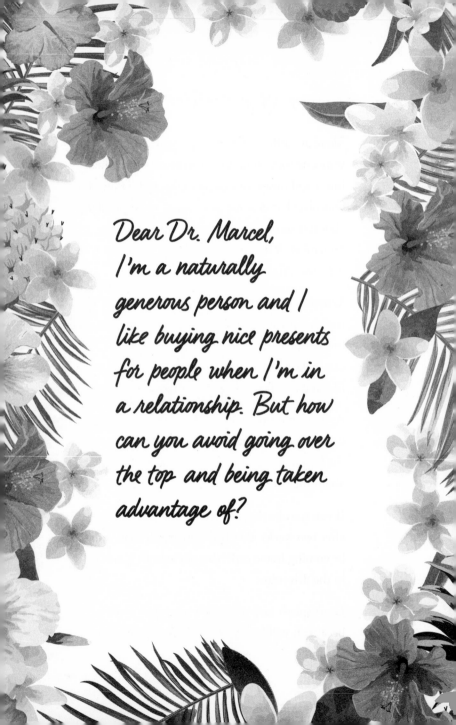

Dear Dr. Marcel,

I'm a naturally generous person and I like buying nice presents for people when I'm in a relationship. But how can you avoid going over the top and being taken advantage of?

There are different levels of presents. You can buy someone something that doesn't cost very much but it will mean a lot to them. Even if it's just a chocolate bar or some sweets they've been talking about, it shows you've been listening and you remember. It doesn't have to be all about the grand gestures early on.

When it comes to your first birthday or Christmas together it's always nice to get them something small but personal, like some jewellery or nice shoes. You can make a note of things they've pointed out they like and get them when the time's right.

As you get deeper into things, like when you've been together for years, you can start getting them the bigger and more valuable presents. It's all about the pace.

If you start buying someone £400 pairs of shoes after two weeks, they'll always expect that. They'll be coming home expecting there to be a new car in the driveway.

Don't splash cash to try and impress someone because it will backfire. You can't buy love, you have to build love. If you buy someone a really expensive watch so they'll like you, it probably won't work and when you split up you ain't getting that watch back.

By doing the smaller things at the start of a relationship you can see if that person wants to be with you for you – or for what they can *get* from you.

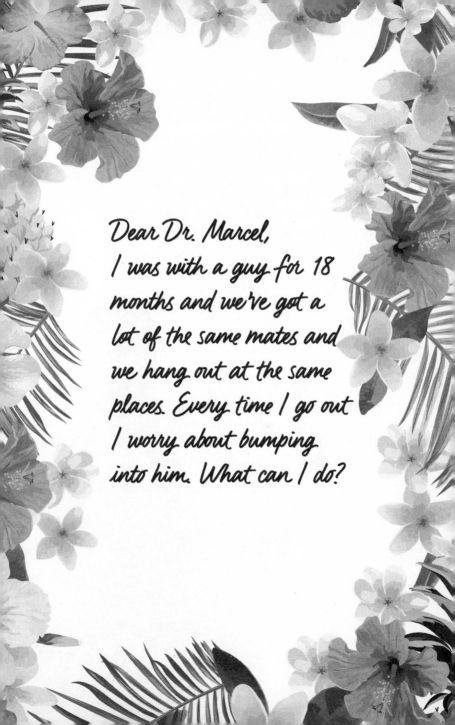

Dear Dr. Marcel,
I was with a guy for 18 months and we've got a lot of the same mates and we hang out at the same places. Every time I go out I worry about bumping into him. What can I do?

♡ ♡ ♡ ♡ ♡ ♡ ♡ ♡ ♡ ♡ ♡ ♡ ♡ ♡

Look, you're going to bump into each other at some point. It's going to happen so bite the bullet and if you see him, say hello and then crack on with your night. You can't avoid certain places just in case your ex is there. If I'd done that back in the day, I'd never have been able to go out. There's nothing you can do. Man up and get on with it.

Dear Dr. Marcel,
it's nearly summer
and I'm gagging for a
holiday. I usually go
with my mates but I'd
really like to go with my
girlfriend this year. The
thing is, we've only been
together for four months.
Is it too soon?

I've known people that have gone away on holiday with someone after they've been together for a couple of weeks, which is well over the top. I reckon if you've been with someone for three or four months, you could go away on a short holiday together. Maybe a long weekend in Ibiza or a city break. Then after six months you can do a proper holiday. By then you'll have built up a strong enough relationship to spend all that time together.

Keep in mind that holidays are a big test and they often prove to be make or break. It's unlikely you'll already be living together by the time you jet off, so it will be the first time you'll be with each other 24/7.

I lived with Gabby for six weeks in the villa and we went from not knowing each other to sleeping in the same bed and waking up next to each other every morning. Within a couple of days I knew whether or not she snored, what she was like in the morning and how she reacted when she was annoyed. We learned a lot about each other very quickly. It can take other couples a year to get to that stage.

Being on holiday
will feel like
you've moved
in together

Being on holiday will feel like you've moved in together. You'll be by each other's side at all times and there's nowhere to escape to. Especially if you're sharing a bedroom and bathroom. That is a massive test. You'll find out so much about them you didn't know, and if they've got one annoying habit you can't stand, it's going to grate on you if it's in your face constantly.

I would recommend just going away for a week the first time you holiday with a partner. Imagine if you get to the end of week one and you're desperate to get away from them and you've still got a whole week to go. Disaster. Do a week to test the water first. Don't jump in to a two weeker until you know they're not going to drive you up the wall.

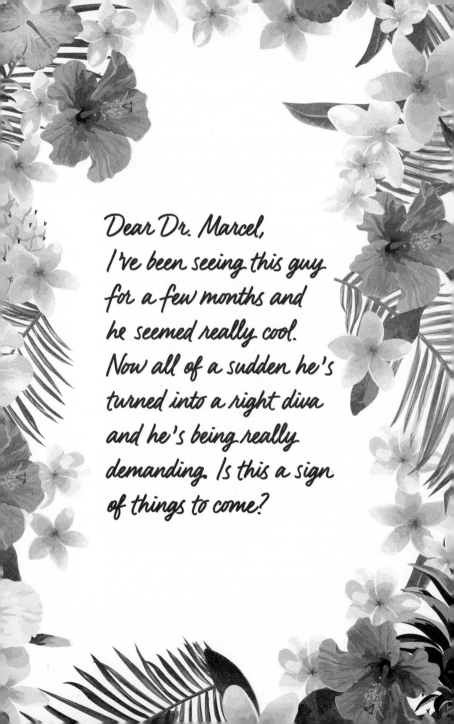

Dear Dr. Marcel,
I've been seeing this guy
for a few months and
he seemed really cool.
Now all of a sudden he's
turned into a right diva
and he's being really
demanding. Is this a sign
of things to come?

I'll level with you; if he's already being demanding this early on in the relationship, it will probably continue. If you're okay with dealing with someone who is high maintenance and you're happy to give them everything they want, there's no problem. If you're not, this is not going to end well.

You could try talking to the guy and flag it up so he knows he's being out of order. But if he doesn't take it on board and that diva behaviour continues, it shows who he really is. Do you really want to put up with that behaviour forever?

If a girl asked me to buy her a £1,000 pair of Louboutins and she got moody when I said no, imagine what she's going to be like about other things. A relationship shouldn't be based on what you can get from someone. It's about give and take.

One of my girl friends went out with this guy who took a car out on finance in her name. They split up and now he's driving the car around town with other girls sat next to him and she's still paying for it. How wrong is that? It's messed up. She won't make that mistake again.

Love can blind you and you may be so infatuated by someone you want to give them the world. But at the end of the day you could end up single with just a very expensive loan agreement for company.

Dear Dr. Marcel,
I've always been
faithful to my girlfriend
but she still gets really
jealous of other girls.
How can I convince her
she's the only one I want?

♡ ♡ ♡ ♡ ♡ ♡ ♡ ♡ ♡ ♡ ♡ ♡ ♡ ♡ ♡

A small amount of jealousy in a relationship is fine. If your girlfriend is going out with her mates and she looks amazing, you're going to worry that other boys are going to try and chat her up. That's only natural. But you've got to trust her. As long as you've got that you'll be fine. Trust should always outweigh jealousy. It sounds like, for whatever reason, your girlfriend is insecure. Maybe someone's cheated on her in the past? Or she's been the cheater?

The only thing you can do is reassure her that you'd never go behind her back and tell her that you're with her for a reason. And that reason is because you don't want to be with anyone else.

At the end of the day, you can't change how she feels, but you can make it better. Trust is something that builds over time so hopefully it will get better.

Dear Dr. Marcel,
my girlfriend and I
are totally in love but
we're bickering all the
time. I'm worried if we
don't stop we'll end up
breaking up over it ...

♡ ♡ ♡ ♡ ♡ ♡ ♡ ♡ ♡ ♡ ♡ ♡ ♡ ♡ ♡

If the bickering is non-stop, it's probably best to have a break for a little bit, otherwise you're going to get to the point where someone says something that the other person really doesn't like and that will be it.

If you've still got strong feelings for each other but you're going through a patch where you're getting on each other's nerves, have some time out for a couple of days. Then get together and talk to see if things can be smoothed over once you've both got cooler heads. Sometimes you need to pull things back before you can start moving forward again.

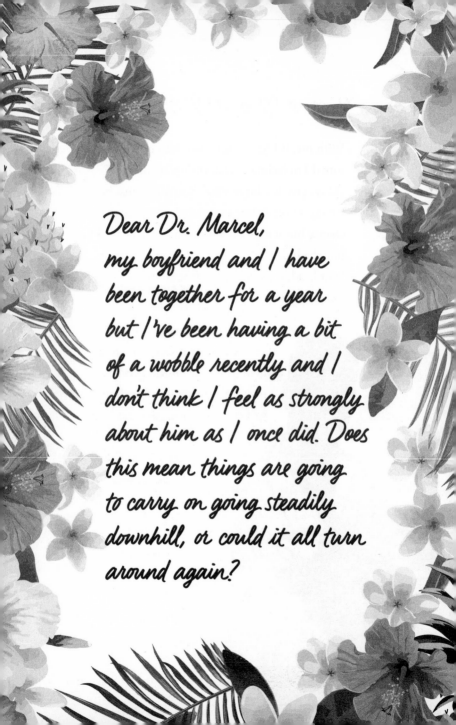

Dear Dr. Marcel,
my boyfriend and I have
been together for a year
but I've been having a bit
of a wobble recently and I
don't think I feel as strongly
about him as I once did. Does
this mean things are going
to carry on going steadily
downhill, or could it all turn
around again?

♡ ♡ ♡ ♡ ♡ ♡ ♡ ♡ ♡ ♡ ♡ ♡ ♡ ♡ ♡

With me, if I have a little wobble and I'm not sure if I'm feeling a relationship anymore, I always give it a bit of time. You might just be having an off day or a bad week. Give things a chance but if that feeling continues, you need to bite the bullet. If the seed has been planted in your head, it could suddenly turn into a massive tree that can't be ignored.

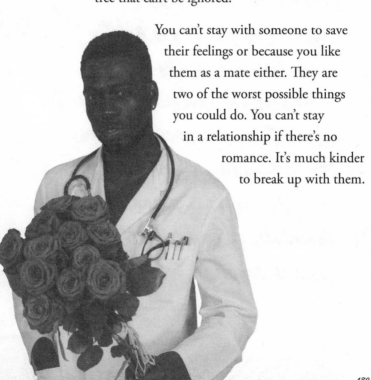

You can't stay with someone to save their feelings or because you like them as a mate either. They are two of the worst possible things you could do. You can't stay in a relationship if there's no romance. It's much kinder to break up with them.

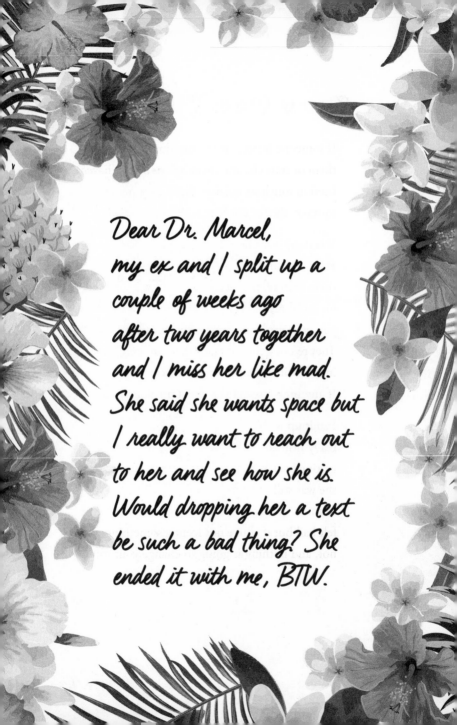

Dear Dr. Marcel,
my ex and I split up a
couple of weeks ago
after two years together
and I miss her like mad.
She said she wants space but
I really want to reach out
to her and see how she is.
Would dropping her a text
be such a bad thing? She
ended it with me, BTW.

If someone finishes with you, do not contact them or start chasing them again. If they haven't been in touch to say they think they've made a mistake, they're not regretting that decision.

You don't want to look like a mug if they don't want you, and you will if you start bombarding them with texts or liking everything they post on social media. If they're going to come back to you, it won't be because you've sent them a text. They're not going to read it and suddenly fall back in love with you. That's not how it works. If anything, you'll push them further away.

I split up with a girl several years ago and I was really firm about the fact that we would not be getting back together. I was very clear cut but she was still constantly on my case and I actually found it quite annoying so I had to ghost her. I felt bad but if you're not feeling something, you're not, and nothing is going to change your mind.

Dear Dr. Marcel,

my boyfriend and I are on the rocks and I reckon we're going to split up any day now. I hate being on my own and I'm thinking of going down the layby route so I've got another guy in place ready to go when the inevitable happens. Some of my mates think that's totally fine and others have said it's bang out of order. What's your take on it?

I hate to say it but I have done the same thing in the past. If things aren't going the way you want them to and you happen to meet someone else in the meantime, sometimes you can't control it if you catch feelings. But you can control what you do about it. I'm not saying for a minute it's fair to stay in a relationship and have someone on the side ready to slide into their place because it's really not. Even if nothing has happened with the new person, it's still going to look like you've cheated and you'll look like a player.

In an ideal world, you would break up with someone as soon as you know it's not working, so you're not leading them on. If you've met someone new, it's not cool to keep them on the side-lines and be grafting them while you're technically still with someone else, even if you don't feel that emotionally involved anymore.

You need to have 'the conversation' with the person you're with before you start pursuing anyone else. How would you feel if you found out someone already had someone else lined up to replace you? It's not nice.

Dear Dr. Marcel,
I've just split up with
my girlfriend after three
years. We're definitely
done but what would be
a respectful amount of
time to wait before I
start dating other girls?

Everyone is different and if someone has broken up with you, it's going to hit you a little bit harder and take longer for you to get your head back in the game and get romantic again. Some people will want to go out and get drunk a lot and sleep with people on the rebound, while others may take some time out to focus before they try to find a new person. It's whatever works for you, innit.

I always think it's good to have between two weeks and a month away from dating after a break-up so you can get your head into the right place before you throw yourself into anything. If you don't, you'll end up feeling crap because you'll have to deal with your emotions at some point, whatever happens.

If you've been in a long-term relationship, of course it can take a lot longer for you to get over someone than if it was just a quick fling, so don't rush yourself. There's no time limit on when you should feel better.

When I split up with my long-term girlfriend I went off the radar for quite a long time.

There's no time limit
on when you should
feel better

Then I realised that I couldn't just sit at home on my own so I started going out and enjoying myself again, but I needed time to reflect and clear my brain.

Be mindful of your ex too. If you split with someone, don't start posting pictures of yourself with someone new on Instagram two days later. It's a horrible thing to do. Be mindful of the other person's feelings. Just because you've moved on it doesn't mean they have. There were two people in that relationship and you've got to consider both of your feelings.

Dear Dr. Marcel,
I think my girlfriend is amazing but I feel like I'm punching above my weight. What can I do to boost my confidence?

Seriously, everyone feels a bit under confident at times. Every single person in the villa had insecurities about different things. It's human nature. There were so many good-looking people in that villa but it didn't matter how beautiful or funny or rich they were, they all had their issues. If you don't feel great about yourself all the time, you're not alone.

You need to keep reminding yourself of what's great about you. Everyone is special and unique and if you're confident and happy, your inner beauty will shine through.

Gabby had a bit of a crisis of confidence in the villa one day and I hated that she felt like that. She's so amazing but she was comparing herself to other people, which is a mistake we all make.

Dear Dr. Marcel,
how can I be a
gentleman like you?

♡ ∨ ♡ ∨ ∨ ♡ ∨ ∨ ♡ ∨ ∨ ♡ ∨ ∨

You know what, the most important thing is to be a nice person. Like, in the villa, if I got myself water, I got everyone water. If I got myself a towel, I got everyone towels. I do that stuff without even thinking.

I always put a lady first and I make sure she's comfortable, and I like to open doors and things. Some people may say it's a bit old fashioned but I think it's nice.

Always be polite and have nice manners, and do things with the best intentions. I'm just as courteous with my mates, my family and even strangers as I am with girls. It's not like I just turn it on when I'm on a date.

Also, be a bit selfless and always have a positive outlook. If you've got that, you'll bring happiness into other people's lives. If you give off positive energy, you'll get positive energy back. You can either live a miserable life or you can live a happy one, so why wouldn't you choose to live a happy one that's filled with love?

Dr. Marcel's Top 5 Love Tips

♡ Be yourself
♡ Always be honest
♡ Communicate
♡ Be understanding
♡ Be kind

Dr. Marcel's Top 5 Date Tips

♡ Be imaginative with venues, and don't go for dinner
♡ Wear garms you feel comfortable in
♡ Make sure you smell good
♡ Ask lots of questions (but not so many you end up looking weird)
♡ Open doors and give compliments

Dr. Marcel's Top 5 Break-Up Rules

♡ Have the conversation face to face somewhere public
♡ Fully listen to what the other person has to say
♡ Be respectful
♡ Don't just ghost someone
♡ Don't post pictures of you and someone new on social media days after you break up. That's a massive pie in the face

Dr. Marcel's Top 5 Ways to Deal with an Argument

♡ Try to stay as calm as possible, even if the other person is kicking off
♡ Don't be extra and blow things out of proportion
♡ Take time out if you need to
♡ Try to see things from the other person's point of view
♡ Talk things through once you've both had a chance to chill out

Dr. Marcel's Top 5 Rules for Dating a Friend's Ex

♡ Don't do it
♡ Don't do it
♡ Don't do it
♡ Don't do it
♡ Don't do it

Dr. Marcel's Top 5 Signs You've Caught Feelings / They're The One

♡ They're the first thing you think about when you wake up
♡ Your heart flips when you see them
♡ You smile when you think about them without even realising it
♡ When you're away from them all you want to do is be with them
♡ You don't make weekend plans because you know you'll be together

My Final Words on Love

What can I say about love except that it's the greatest thing in the world?

Love has the power to uplift, heal, change and break people. It's the most powerful emotion we have so make sure you embrace it when you feel it. I love love.

I hope that if you don't already have someone special in your life that appreciates you and treats you the way you deserve to be treated, you find them very, very soon.

Lots of love,

Dr. Marcel XXX

Acknowledgements

Many thanks to all the people who made this book happen. My agents Matt, Chloe and Georgia at Loco Talent, Annabel and Laura from PFD, Natalie, Nathan and Madiya from Blink, and Jordan Paramor. Lewis, Dan, Henry, Coco, Chuck, Tom, Andy, Sarah and all the team at ITV for giving me the opportunity to go on *Love Island* in the first place. And my mum, dad, sister and grandparents for raising me so well and helping me become the gentleman I am today. I'd also like to thank all my friends who have been there for me throughout the good times and the bad. And, of course, thank you to you lot for all your incredible support. I know you were with me every step of the way while I was in the villa and you helped to make it such an amazing ride.